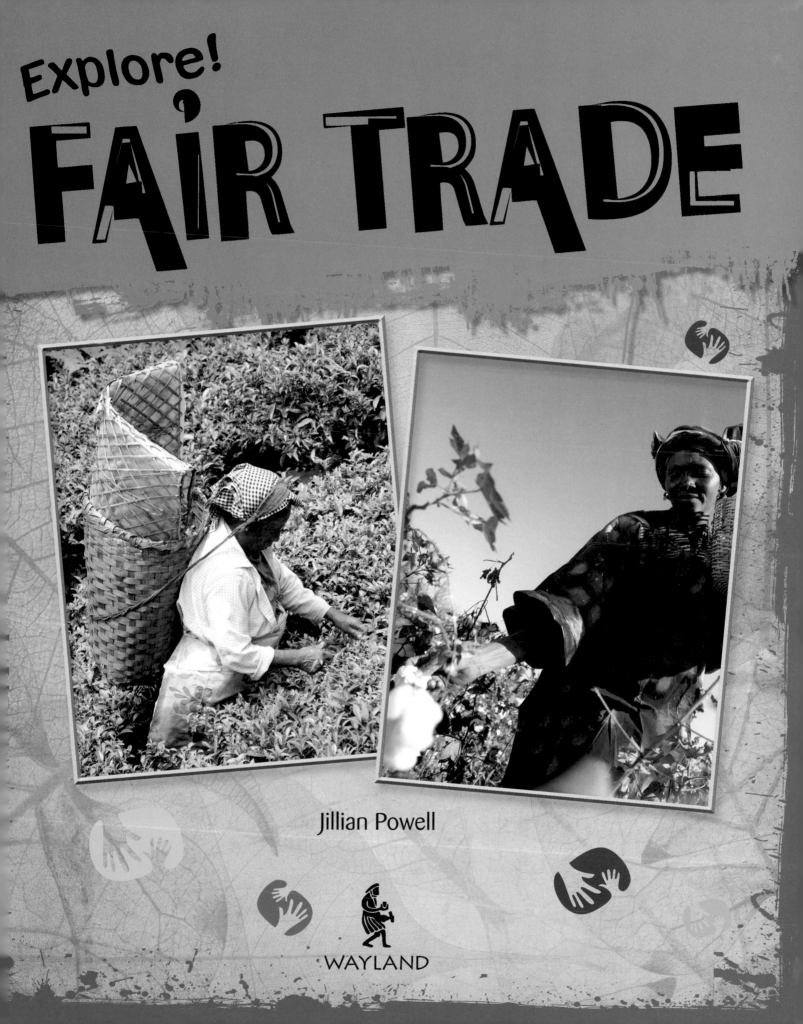

Explore! FAIR TRADE

Jillian Powell

WAYLAND

First published in 2012 by Wayland
Copyright © Wayland 2012
Reprinted in 2012

Wayland
338 Euston Road
London NW1 3BH

Wayland Australia
Level 17/207 Kent Street
Sydney, NSW 2000

Editors: Victoria Brooker and Julia Adams
Designer: Elaine Wilkinson
Picture Researcher: Shelley Noronha
Illustrations for step-by-steps: Peter Bull

British Library Cataloguing in Publication Data

Fair trade. -- (Explore!)
   1. Competition, Unfair--Juvenile literature.
   I. Series
   338.5'22-dc23

ISBN: 978 0 7502 6847 9

Printed in China

Wayland is a division of Hachette Children's
Books, an Hachette UK company

www.hachette.co.uk

Picture acknowledgements:
The author and publisher would like to thank the
following agencies and people for allowing these
pictures to be reproduced:

Cover (top and bottom left, 16) Simon Rawles
(top right) © Joerg Boethling / Alamy
bottom (left) Vetta collection/iStockphoto;
p 2 (right) Bintou Dembele (left and 7 top)
PavelSvoboda/Shutterstock; p4 © Photoshot; p5
(top) Divine Chocolate (bottom) © imagebroker/
Alamy; p6 (top) Swapan/ Shutterstock (bottom)
HYPERLINK "http://www.shutterstock.
com/gallery-503215p1.html" Darrin Henry
Shutterstock; p7 (top) Bintou Dembele (middle)
Rehan Qureshi/Shutterstock (bottom left) Tristan
tan/Shutterstock (bottom right) Maks Narodenko/
Shutterstock; p8 (middle) Shutterstock; p 9 (left)
Alasdair James/iStockphoto (middle) Marcus
Lyons, (right) Lasse Kristensen/Shutterstock; p
10 Jean-Daniel Sudres/Hemis/Corbis; p 11 (top)
Simon Rawles, (bottom) AFP/Getty Images; p12
Amit Dave/X01413/Reuters/Corbis; p 13 (top)
westphalia/iStockphoto
 (bottom) Divine Chocolate; p 14 © Bruce
Coleman/Photoshot; 15 (top) Nigel Cattlin/
Visuals Unlimited/Corbis (bottom) Divine
Chocolate; p 16 Simon Rawles; 17 (top and
bottom) Fair Trade; p18 and p19: Conserve
India; p 20 © MOHSIN RAZA/Reuters/Corbis;
p 21 (top) © Rahat Dar/epa/Corbis; (bottom)
R-O-M-A, Shutterstock; p 22 Divine Chocolate;
p 23 (top) © Ocean/Corbis; p 23 (bottom) Ray
Roberts/Rex Features; p 24 © Simon Kimber/
Demotix/Demotix/Demotix/Corbis; p25 (top)
Marco Secchi/Rex Features (bottom) YURI
CORTEZ/AFP/Getty Images

Contents

Fair trade for all

Fair trade is a way of trading which helps people who farm or make goods in developing countries sell their products at a fair price. Developing countries are countries where many people still work on the land and live on very little money. Fair trade pays them a fair price for their produce so they can earn more and work their way out of poverty.

Machinery helps farmers in developed countries to keep their prices low.

Why is trade not fair?

Farmers in developing countries often find it hard to match the prices for goods that growers from developed countries can offer. In developed countries, farmers can afford to buy machinery that keeps their costs down. They may also be given money grants by governments to help them. In developing countries, farmers can face challenges such as mountainous land or a climate that brings hurricanes or drought. Often they cannot afford to buy machinery or use the latest technology. This makes their costs higher so they cannot match the low prices offered by the farmers in developed countries.

The Fairtrade premium pays for community projects like this water pump at a school in Ghana, West Africa.

The Fairtrade premium
The fair trade system pays a fair price, but it also pays extra money – called the Fairtrade premium – to support community projects such as wells for clean water, schools or health clinics. It encourages safe working practices and farming methods that will help to improve the environment.

FAIRTRADE

Fair trade organisations
The World Fair Trade Organisation (WFTO) was set up in 1989 to make global trading fairer. Members include farmers, growers, producers and traders from all over the world. Another global network, Fairtrade Labelling Organisations (FLO) International, awards the Fairtrade mark to produce that meets international standards for fair trade. There are many smaller fair trade organisations, such as cooperatives, which are groups of farmers working together to provide goods to sell under the Fairtrade mark.

Global market

Thousands of goods are grown or produced by Fairtrade farmers and growers around the world. They include fruit, vegetables, rice, nuts, honey, tea, coffee, sugar, spices, wine, cocoa, flowers, gold, clothing, homewares, beauty products and sports balls.

Sugar cane – Malawi, South Africa

Farmers in the Kasinthula cooperative grow Fairtrade sugar. They have used the Fairtrade premium to pay for clean drinking water and electricity in workers' homes and to fund schools and a community health clinic.

Coffee – Costa Rica

The Coocafé coffee cooperative has over 3,500 farmers producing over 4,000 tonnes of Fairtrade coffee beans each year on small farms. It employs or helps around 15,000 local people. The coffee is grown under the shade of other trees, providing a wildlife habitat and protecting the rainforest.

Tea - Makaibari, India

Fairtrade tea is grown organically without using chemical fertilisers and pesticides. The tea bushes grow on mixed plantations with other plants and forest trees which provide a wildlife habitat. The Fairtrade premium has been used to bring electricity to villages, and fund schools and health clinics.

Cotton - Gujarat, India

The Agrocol Pure and Fair Cotton Grower's Association has nearly 2,000 members, growing 6,000 hectares of organic cotton. Without Fairtrade, cotton pickers worked long hours for little pay and had health problems caused by harmful chemical pesticides.

Cacao - Ghana, West Africa

The Kuapa Kokoo cocoa cooperative represents almost 50,000 cacao growers, growing cacao beans, which are used to make chocolate, on small family farms where cacao grows with other trees.

Bananas - Dominican Republic

The Banelino cooperative has over 340 members. The Fairtrade premium has helped fund schools and medical clinics close to banana farms. It also funds a sports curriculum to tackle problems of drugs and alcohol amongst the young.

Bananas

Bananas are an important part of life for the people of the Windward Islands in the Caribbean. Around half the population rely on income from the banana crop for their living, and bananas make up half of all exports.

The problem with bananas

Bananas are grown on small, family-run farms, but as the price of bananas has fallen worldwide, it is getting harder for farmers to support their families. They can spend more than half their earnings on fertilisers, pesticides, packaging and transport from their farms to the docks. The land is steep and hilly, and the tropical climate can bring damaging hurricanes. Crops can also suffer damage from drought or outbreaks of disease, which can reduce harvests by up to a half.

This woman is washing and packing bananas for export.

The Fairtrade market

It has become increasingly hard for farmers to compete with the big, international companies that can produce cheap 'dollar bananas' (bananas grown for the US market). These have been grown on large plantations in South America and Africa, which have lower labour costs and make more use of chemical fertilisers and pesticides. Fairtrade helps farmers to compete with these bigger companies. In return for Fairtrade prices and premiums, they agree to use environmentally-friendly practices, such as not using genetically modified (GM) seed, and making sure that plastic used to protect banana trees is recycled or disposed of responsibly.

Community projects

The Fairtrade premium helps to fund community projects on the islands including hospitals and healthcare clinics, clean water supplies, school buses, desks and chairs for primary schools, and improvement to roads and bridges. It helps farmers to improve the quality of their produce, and to buy fertilisers, packaging materials and trucks for transporting crops. It can also help when crops are damaged or destroyed by hurricanes, by funding work to repair damage and replant trees.

Hurricane Dean destroyed crops on the Windward islands in 2007.

Water

Fair trade is not just about people and communities. It is also about improving the local environment. Fair trade organisations work with local communities to tackle problems such as lack of access to clean, safe water.

Dirty water

Over a billion people in developing countries lack access to clean water. In parts of Africa and Asia, women and children can spend up to six hours a day walking to fetch water for their families, allowing them less time for work or schooling. Dirty water causes 80 per cent of diseases in developing countries and over 2 million people, mainly children, die from them each year. As the world's population grows and we need more and more water, the amount available for each person is expected to fall by a third by 2025.

Women often have to walk miles a day to fetch clean water for their families or businesses.

12

Saving water

Fairtrade works with farmers to save and recycle water. In the western highlands of Kenya, Fairtrade flower farmers protect local water supplies by growing flowers using hydroponics, a method of growing plants without soil, using water containing nutrients. This can use up to 90 per cent less water than growing in soil. They also recycle water for use on other crops, and prevent pollution of water sources from chemical pesticides. Finlay Flowers in Kericho, Kenya, have created wetland areas (areas of lakes and marshes) on their flower farms to recycle and purify water used in their packing houses.

Farming uses 70 per cent of available fresh water.

Funding development

Many Fairtrade farmers and growers working in regions where access to clean water is a problem, use the Fairtrade premium to help pay for digging wells, installing pumps or piping clean water to people's homes and businesses.

A Fairtrade brand of bottled water, 'Ethos', has also been created to help fund water, sanitation and hygiene education programmes. For every bottle sold in the U.S., five cents goes towards development funds.

The Fairtrade premium has helped fund piped water for families living in Ghana.

Chocolate

air trade supports sustainable methods of farming, which also helps wildlife and the environment. Buying Fairtrade chocolate helps to support sustainable methods of cacao farming.

A cacao plantation in Malaysia.

Growing cacao

Chocolate is made from cacao beans. Traditionally, cacao beans have been grown on small plantations where a variety of trees provide shade and habitat for birds and other wildlife. But many cacao farmers have begun growing cacao trees as a single crop on large plantations in full sun. These trees produce more beans but they also need more water, pesticides and fertilisers to keep them healthy and disease-free.

Coconut palms shade cacao on this plantation in the Philippines.

Mixed plantations

Most Fairtrade chocolate is organic and shade-grown, which means the cacao trees grow under the canopy of taller rainforest trees. Shade-grown cacao trees produce smaller crops but the trees live longer and produce more flavoursome beans. Farmers can receive income from other crops including rubber, Brazil nuts, limes and chillies. There are also many benefits for wildlife and the environment.

Sustainable farming

Shade trees help to keep the cacao trees healthy. Leaves from shade trees fall to the ground where they break down, returning nutrients to the soil and discouraging weed growth. Soil nutrients fertilise cacao trees and help them resist disease. Shade from surrounding trees help to keep moisture in the soil reducing the need for water. Shade trees also provide a habitat for many species including migratory birds.

Fair trade means fair pay and working conditions on cacao plantations.

Cotton

The Fairtrade cotton market shows how some of the main goals of fair trade work in practice.

Supports small producers
Around 20,000 farmers belong to the Agrocel cotton farmers cooperative in India. Fairtrade means that they can rely on a fair wage and regular work.

A fair price
Fairtrade buyers pay farmers up to 20 per cent more for their cotton crop than they would typically receive on the open market, as it can be sold for a higher price.

Protects traditional skills
Fairtrade cotton is hand picked and spun, and woven on hand looms. Many skills including embroidery, crochet, hand beading and hand block printing are used to design and make cotton clothing, bags and homewares.

Information and communication
There is regular communication and open information all the way through production to sale, from the cotton farmers and workers through to buyers and shoppers.

Good working conditions

Fair working hours and conditions are agreed for workers. Without Fairtrade, cotton pickers had to work long hours for very little pay and had health problems caused by using chemical pesticides.

Equal opportunities/ No child labour

Fairtrade means cotton farms offer equal opportunities regardless of race, caste, religion or gender, and do not employ children, who are used for cheap labour on cotton farms in some countries.

Advertising and promotion

Fashion shows, photography shoots and celebrity support help to raise awareness of Fairtrade cotton and how it improves the lives of cotton farmers.

Development

Growers are offered training and help such as advance payments for orders. Regular orders mean they can plan ahead.

Sustainable farming

Fairtrade cotton is grown organically, without harmful chemical fertilisers and pesticides, using environmentally-friendly methods and dyes. Farmers do not use genetically modified (GM) seed. They use recycled or biodegradable packaging and sea transport rather than air transport, as it produces less carbon emission (CO_2) that contributes to climate change.

Footballs

In Sialkot, Pakistan, nearly half the population, around 40,000 workers, rely on making footballs for their living. Many of the world's footballs are made here. But in the past, the industry has used low paid piece-workers, including women and children, working long hours in poorly run stitching centres.

An experienced worker can stitch two or three footballs a day.

Work and wages

Fairtrade means that employers must agree to pay workers fair pay, at least the national minimum wage (a minimum amount set by the government) and provide them with secure jobs. On average, wages have increased by around 50 per cent. Fairtrade also prevents children working in factories and provides proper health and safety measures in the workplace. A number of small stitching centres have been set up, near to family homes, making it easier for women to get to work. Employers have to provide good lighting, fresh air and access to drinking water.

Choosing to play with a Fairtrade football can make a real difference to people's lives.

Stitching centres

A Fairtrade football can cost little more than one sold under a big brand name, but it can make a real difference to the workers who make it. The footballs are handmade from leather patches that are stamped out and stitched together. One worker can stamp out patches for between 300–400 footballs a day. The patches and the inside casings then go to stitching centres to be sewn together into balls. Experienced workers can stitch two or three footballs a day, which are then sent to the factory to be checked and packed for shipping.

Development projects

The Fairtrade premium is used to fund community and development projects, including healthcare schemes, and schools for children, which are often run alongside the stitching centres where their parents are working. Fairtrade is also supporting young people in Sialkot by providing small loans to help them start up new businesses such as opening video shops or snooker halls.

Index

Explore!

The world of chocolate
Cocoa beans
The chocolate factory
Putting chocolate on the map
Fairtrade chocolate
Ancient food of the gods
Chocolate reaches Europe
Birth of the chocolate bar
Is chocolate good for you?
Chocolate celebrations
Chocolate-dipped strawberries
Yummy careers
Facts and figures

978 0 7502 6848 6

The circus is in town!
The first circuses
Travelling circuses
Traditional circuses today
Animals in the ring
The show stoppers
Circus performers
Learn to juggle
The great state circuses
Contemporary circuses
Life behind the scenes
Circus careers
Facts and figures

978 0 7502 6849 3

Fair trade for all
Global market
History of fair trade
Bananas
Water
Chocolate
Cotton
Improving lives
Footballs
Debating fair trade
Raising awareness
Make it fair trade!
Facts and figures

978 0 7502 6847 9

What are fairgrounds?
Theme parks
Fairgrounds in the past
Fairground people
The attractions
All around the World
Fairground art and music
How do roller coasters work?
Fairground sensations
Make a fairground ride
Zoah's story
Fairground safety
Facts and figures

978 0 7502 6850 9

London life
The birth of London
Medieval and Tudor London
Enter the Victorian Age
London under attack
City transport
Make a London bus
Sport in London
Fashionable London
Learn all about it!
The people of London
The River Thames
Facts and figures

978 0 7502 6846 2

Where in the World?
Forest layers
Rainforest glider
Feeding and food chains
Why are rainforests important?
Rainforest people
New arrivals
Rainforest produce
Rainforest recipe
Paradise lost
Rainforest conservation
Interview with a campaigner
Facts and figures

978 0 7502 6845 5

WAYLAND